Seashore

Written by Emily Bone

Illustrated by Cinzia Battistel

Designed by Anna Gould

Seashore consultant: Zoë Simmons
Reading consultant: Alison Kelly

A seashore is where land meets the sea. Lots of animals and plants live there.

Cormorant

Curlew

Sand is tiny pieces of broken shell and rock.

Speckled crab

Lapwings

Seals

Plover and chicks

Sometimes a seashore
is covered in water.

Black headed gulls

At other times, it is bare.
Birds hunt for food.

Oystercatchers

Clam

Pools of water collect between rocks on some seashores. Animals live in the pools.

Limpet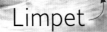

Shrimp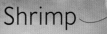

Blenny

Mussel

Shore crab

Sea stickleback

Starfish

Periwinkle

Many seashore creatures have
hard shells.

Hermit crabs find old shells
and live inside them.

Babylonia shell

Hermit crab

Barnacles attach themselves to rocks.
They stick out their legs to catch food.

Legs →

Cowries crawl along the seabed
looking for food.

Cowrie

Sea squirt

Different plants grow on the seashore.

Beachgrass

Sea holly

Seaweed grows on rocks.
Sometimes it washes up
on the beach.

Thrift grows
between rocks.

Some seashore creatures have long arms called tentacles.

Lion's mane jellyfish have tentacles that sting.

A fish is killed by the sting. Then the jellyfish eats it.

Sea anemones sting creatures that swim into their tentacles.

Shrimp   Sea anemone

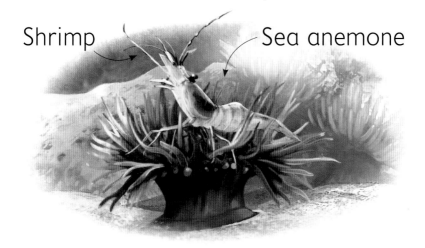

Nautiluses use their tentacles to grab food.

Nautilus

Crab

Other seashore creatures have ways to protect themselves from attackers.

Porcupinefish are covered in sharp spikes. They puff up if they're attacked.

Sealion

A cuttlefish squirts out a cloud of ink to hide in.

Cuttlefish

Shark

Sea urchins have long spikes on their bodies.

Lots of birds live by the sea.

Pelicans dive
under the water
and scoop up fish
in their beaks.

Herring

Other birds find food on the beach.

Redshanks have long beaks to
pull creatures out of the sand.

Crab

Turnstones look
under stones and
seaweed for food.

17

Puffins are birds that make nests on some seashores.

They dig a burrow in the ground.

The mother lays an egg in the burrow. She sits on the egg to keep it warm.

A chick hatches. The parents collect fish to feed to the chick.

The chick grows bigger.
It leaves the burrow.

Sea otters look for food in the sea.

They dive down to pick
up sea creatures.

They collect
rocks too.

Clams

An otter lays a rock on its tummy.

It hits a clam on the rock
to break it open.

It pulls out the insides of
the clam and eats them.

Some seashores are very, very cold.

Seals have thick, fat bodies
to keep them warm.

Weddell seal

Baby seals are
called pups.

Penguins dive
into the icy sea
to catch food.

Adélie
penguin

Their feathers are covered in oil.
This keeps out the cold water.

Antarctic
silverfish

23

Other seashores are very warm. Lots of creatures live in the warm sea.

Seahorse

Parrotfish

Coral is a type of animal. It clings onto rocks.

Moorish idol

Giant clam

Butterfly
fish

Clownfish

Starfish

Sea turtles live in warm seas.
They eat sea creatures.

Hawksbill sea turtle

Jellyfish

Sea
sponge

They come onto beaches to lay eggs.

They bury their eggs in the sand.

Baby turtles hatch out.
They crawl back to
the sea.

A mudskipper is a type of fish that lives in and out of the sea.

It uses its fins to move on land and swim when it's in water.

Some creatures live under the sand.

Lugworms leave piles
of sand as they dig down.

Ghost crabs live in burrows.
They come out to catch
food at night.

Jellyfish

Sometimes there are storms with very strong winds.

There are big crashing waves too.

Lots of things are washed
onto the beach.

Mussel shells

Cuttlefish
bone

Heart urchin shell

Blue jellyfish

31

The sea is calm after a storm.
Birds feed on the things that
were washed up.

Herring gull

Digital retouching by John Russell